Sow and

KU-198-459

Plants for presents, vegetables and
herbs to eat, window boxes and
bottle gardens – all these can be
yours even if you don't have
a garden, and *Sow and Grow*
tells you how.

Cover illustration by Desmond Clover

Sow and Grow

Eileen Totten

Illustrated by S. F. Martin

Evans Brothers Limited London

Published by Evans Brothers Limited
Montague House, Russell Square,
London WC1

© Evans Brothers Limited 1973
First published 1973

Set in 12 on 14 point Baskerville and
printed in Great Britain by
Cox & Wyman Limited,
London, Reading and Fakenham.

CSD ISBN 0 237 44714 2   PRA 3483'
PB   ISBN 0 237 44715 0

Contents

Acknowledgment

I should like to thank Mr. L. B. Lowries, till recently Adviser on Rural Studies to Birmingham Education Authority, for his help and advice in preparing this book. And to thank Miss Jane Headley who typed the manuscript.

How you start

You can start quite early growing things, in your house or in your Dad's garden. You don't need a lot of money or a lot of tools to grow bulbs and other small plants.

Most children start off with something they can grow at home in the house. Later in the book I will be telling you how to plant bulbs and how to grow pot plants. If you don't have a garden, you can try growing plants in window-boxes or in tubs which you can stand outside.

You can grow plants from seeds which you buy at the shop. Or you can try growing from pips and stones left over from fruit you have just eaten! Sometimes it is best to buy a plant from a shop. Then, when it grows bigger, you can divide it, or take cuttings to give to your friends.

Grow something that will show good results quite quickly. Don't choose plants which are very delicate and need special care – at least at first! This is why bulbs are good to start with. And I will also be telling you later about pot plants, and some herbs and vegetables that are not hard to grow.

You will only need a very few tools when you start gardening indoors. Many firms make today's tools in light materials so you will be able to choose things that are not too heavy for you. You can ask at the gardening shop or centre if there are any special tools for children. Otherwise, choose tools that feel comfortable in your hands. Make sure they are not too heavy or too big, and that they are strong but light.

You need only three tools to start with, for gardening in pots, window-boxes or tubs. These are: a *hand fork*, a *hand trowel*, and a *watering can*. A plastic watering can might be best to begin with. Of course, you will also need pots and compost or peat in which to grow things, but I will be telling you more about that later. Later on, too, you might ask your Dad if you can grow things in a small patch of his garden. Then you will need to use other gardening tools, too. I will be explaining about this in the last chapter.

You should always look after your tools, clean them and put them away after you have used them. This won't be difficult at first with only three things to look after! But it's a good habit to get into for the time when you may be a fully-grown gardener!

This book starts with the easiest things to grow, and goes on to more difficult things to try. I hope you enjoy working through it. And I hope everything you grow is a success.

Growing bulbs in the house

What you need

A bulb
A plant pot
A pebble

Bulb fibre or peat
Water
A large bowl

Start at first with one bulb in a simple pot. Choose your bulb in September and plant it straight away if you want results around February. You can choose hyacinth, crocus or snowdrop bulbs. All of these will grow well in a pot or bowl. A daffodil bulb on its own will not make a very good show.

You need the large bowl I have mentioned for mixing the fibre or sedge peat in water. It might be a good idea to spread newspaper on the table or floor before you do this. Pour the water, little by little, on to the fibre or peat and mix it together with your hands. It will be ready when you can squeeze a few drops of water out of it.

If you use a clay pot for your bulb you will need to put

a pebble or small piece of broken pot over the drainage hole. You can put a few dry leaves on top of this, and then pack in fibre half-way up the pot.

Now it is time to plant the bulb. Put it on the fibre, so its top, the pointed end, just sticks up level with the rim of the pot. Then pack more fibre tightly round the bulb till the pot is almost full. The peat or fibre should reach to about 1·3 cm. from the rim of the pot. Water the bulb well.

Now is the time when the bulb must go away in the dark for eight or ten weeks. It needs this time to grow strong roots before it starts flowering. A good place might be a cupboard which is not used too often, or an attic where you can put a box over the pot to keep the light out. Make sure it is a cool place that you choose, too. Don't keep looking at the bulb, or you will let the light in. But do water it from time to time. Feel the fibre to see if it is too dry.

After ten weeks, your bulb should show a strong shoot just over 2·5 cm. long. You can bring the pot into the daylight now and put it on a windowsill. Make sure the bulb gets plenty of light, but not too much heat. The bulb should grow slowly and not be forced. Never put it beside a fire, for instance.

Water the bulbs so that the fibre or peat is always moist. And turn the plant round once a week so it won't lean over one way, to get to the sunlight. When it starts to flower, you can push a little stick into the fibre. Then tie the flower stalk loosely to it, to support it.

This is how to grow one bulb in a pot. Growing bulbs in

a bowl is very much the same. If you use a bowl, then you must put pieces of charcoal in the bottom instead of a pebble. When you water bulbs in a bowl there will be no drainage hole for surplus water to run away. Instead, you must tilt the bowl carefully to one side to let the water run away.

If you want to plant more than one bulb in your bowl, then choose bulbs all of one kind – all daffodil or all hyacinth, or all crocus, but not a mixture. You need a pot about 12·6 cm. to grow one hyacinth, or six crocus, for instance. You will need a larger pot for three daffodils. Put the bulbs in the bowl so they are almost touching each other and pack the peat firmly around each one, so they stay in position. Don't try to cram too many bulbs into one bowl – you will see just what is a good number to put in.

Some bulbs you can grow in water, without any soil at all! The one to try is the paper-white narcissus. Buy the bulb at the gardening shop.

What you need

Narcissus bulb
Pebbles

A bowl to hold the bulb
Water

Put a layer of pebbles in the bottom of your bowl. Then put the bulb or bulbs on top. Add some more pebbles until you can see the pointed end of the bulbs sticking up.

Now put in enough water to just touch the bottom of the bulbs. You must keep it always at this level by checking each day and adding a little water if it is necessary.

Now you can put the bowl in a sunny place, in the window. If you plant the bulbs in October they will take about eight or nine weeks to flower. But if you plant in December they should be out in three or four weeks. They flower naturally in the spring. So the later you plant them, the less time you will have to wait.

Here are a few special tips on different types of bulbs. If you want to grow daffodils always buy large bulbs and give them plenty of time in the dark. You can get quite good results with second size hyacinths, though. Crocuses should be kept in the dark till just before Christmas. Snowdrops should be left in the dark until the leaves have grown quite a lot – if they are brought out too early they may not flower. If you want to encourage a bulb, such as a hyacinth one, which is a bit slower than the others, make it a little paper 'hat'.

All the bulbs I have mentioned here are strong and hardy. They should grow well. Remember that small bulbs especially should be kept cold till they are nearly ready to flower.

Bulbs make nice Christmas presents for friends or your family. If you want them to flower this early, you must buy specially prepared bulbs from the shop. They don't cost much to grow, but people will know they are really a present from *you*.

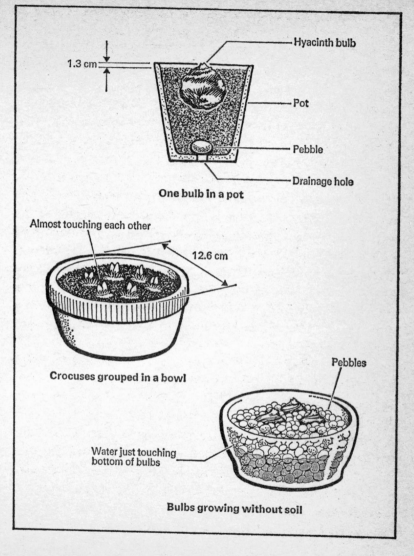

Hyacinth bulb

1.3 cm

Pot

Pebble

Drainage hole

One bulb in a pot

Almost touching each other

12.6 cm

Crocuses grouped in a bowl

Pebbles

Water just touching
bottom of bulbs

Bulbs growing without soil

Growing plants in pots

It is quite easy to grow some plants in pots if you just spend a minute or two each day. This means seeing if the plant needs watering, turning it round every day, and seeing whether it has grown so much it needs a larger pot.

You can grow pot plants from seed, but the easiest way to begin with is to get someone you know to give you a small plant or seedling. You can buy these at the gardening shop, too. Later on in the book, I will tell you how to grow plants from seed.

What you need
A baby plant
A pot about 7·6 cm.
A watering can

Potting soil
A saucer
A pebble

A good plant to try growing at first is the coleus. This has bright red leaves and is a kind of nettle, though it doesn't sting. Actually, it makes a pretty plant and is a popular one. Another plant you might try to begin with is the Busy Lizzy, or gloxinia. Both of these have pretty flowers. The Busy Lizzy grows fast, as its name suggests, so you will have to keep a close eye on it.

You need to buy special potting soil, because soil from the garden is not really rich enough. One kind you might buy is John Innes potting compost, or you could try a 'no soil' compost such as Levington or Kerrimure (ICI) or Arthur Bowers compost. You can buy these at pet and garden shops, usually.

Wash your pot carefully and dry it. If it is a new pot let it soak first for a few hours. Then put a pebble over the drainage hole, just as you did when you were growing bulbs. If you use a clay pot, put a small lump of soil or moss in the bottom. Then put some soil in the pot. Now, you can pick up your baby plant and hold it in your left hand. Make sure the roots are hanging down straight into the pot. Then pick up soil in your other hand and pack it carefully around the roots, a bit at a time.

You need to fill your pot to about 6 mm. from the top. Then make the soil settle by giving the pot a firm tap on the table. You must make sure the little plant is now firmly in position. Now you can water the plant well – you could try standing it in a sink so that the water runs away easily. The last step is to put your pot on a saucer, and then find a windowsill which is warm and sunny. This will be a good place to stand your new plant.

It isn't really the last thing to do, of course, because you will have to see your plant has everything it needs. You don't have to water it each day – too much water can be as bad as none at all. Plants in plastic pots need less water than those in clay pots. Water the plant when the soil is nearly dry and then give it a proper watering as you did right at the beginning. If the leaves start to wilt and go limp, the plant needs water at once.

At some time – quite soon if you are growing a Busy Lizzy – your plant will outgrow its first pot. Then you will need to re-pot it, to give the roots more room. You will need a pot about 12·6 cm. in diameter. Again, put a pebble over the drainage hole; then add potting soil.

Take the plant very gently out of its old pot, with some soil still clinging to the roots. Don't shake this off. Now, re-plant in the new pot, just as you did the first time. Press the soil down quite firmly and re-fill the new pot to about 6 mm. from the top. Now water the plant again.

You can re-pot plants several times like this, for as they grow they need more food. You could also feed the plant special fertiliser which you can buy. Read the instructions carefully before you give any of this to the plant.

Don't forget to turn your plant round quite often so that each part gets the same amount of light. And pick off any dead leaves. Keep the soil free from weeds.

Other plants you might like to grow inside are: Clarkia, dwarf marigolds, dwarf nasturtiums. Some time, you may want to help someone else start a plant collection. Then you can take a cutting from your plant for them. I'll be telling you how to take cuttings in a later chapter.

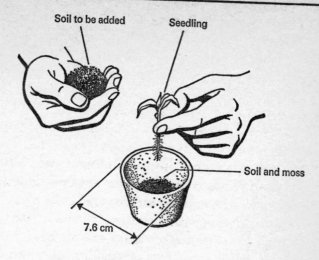

Soil to be added

Seedling

Soil and moss

7.6 cm

Planting a seedling

A plant collection

Sow and grow

Now that you can grow flowers from plants and bulbs, you might try sowing seeds in pots. This is more difficult than the things you have done so far. Instead of starting with a plant you are starting with a seed which can be very small. You will find that most seeds need special heat and care. Try growing coleus seeds first of all. Primulas and cinerarias also grow quite well from seeds.

What you need
Coleus seeds
Seed compost
An elastic band

A flower pot or seed box
A plastic bag

You can buy your seeds at the gardening shop. You need seed compost which is sterile so that the only shoots that grow will be your plants, and not weeds! When you first start growing things you may find it hard to tell the plants you want from the weeds.

Fill your seed box or flower pot with the compost, to just about 1·3 cm. from the top. Then check the compost is level. Scatter the seeds, not all in one place, but quite thinly, on top of the compost. Then shake more seed compost thinly over the seeds, just to hold them gently in place. If the compost seems rather dry, water very carefully and let the surplus water drain out.

Now you can help your seeds to grow quickly by putting the pot or box gently inside a plastic bag. This helps to keep the seeds warm and away from draughts. You can tie up the opening of the bag with the elastic band. Then find a warm place for the seeds – above a radiator, if you have central heating, or on a windowsill. Some people have even grown seeds in the airing cupboard! But you'd better ask Mum about this first.

Because of the warmth inside the bag, condensation might collect on the sides of it. If this happens, you can untie the bag, turn it inside out and then put it back over the seeds. Soon, you will see little green shoots beginning to appear in the soil and your plants will have started to grow.

Another way to help seeds grow and keep them warm is to cover the pot with glass. Then put paper over the top to keep the seeds in the dark.

After a day or two, the new seedlings will need plenty of light, so take them out of the airing cupboard if you have kept them there till now. You can also open the neck of the plastic bag to give the plants some air now they are growing quite strongly. Soon you will have to remove

the plastic bag altogether. The seedlings will need all the
the light they can get on a windowsill.

But you can't let all the seedlings grow like this without
moving them or getting rid of the weak ones. Soon there
will be no room in your pot or box for them to grow
properly. The first thing is to gently prick out any shoots
which look weak or sickly. Then the others will have a
better chance. But be careful how you do this. Try not to
disturb the good seedlings or the seed compost around
them. This is because the little root hairs are so fine and
easily hurt.

Let the good seedlings grow a little longer before pricking
them out into larger pots. When it is time to do this, again
you must disturb the roots of the new plants as little as
possible. Get your new pots ready with the same seed
compost as you have been using – make sure they are not
too big for the little plants. Then use a pencil to very
gently ease the seedlings, one by one, out of their first pot
and into their new homes. Try to keep as much compost
around the roots of each one as you move it. Then replant
it just as carefully.

Make sure the plant is kept sufficiently watered, stays
warm and away from draughts. By this stage you shouldn't
need the plastic bag any more. Your new plant or plants
should be strong enough to grow up with just a little care
from you.

Watch the plant each day, because it is always interesting
to see how things grow. And also check that the compost
is not too dry and that the pot is still big enough for the

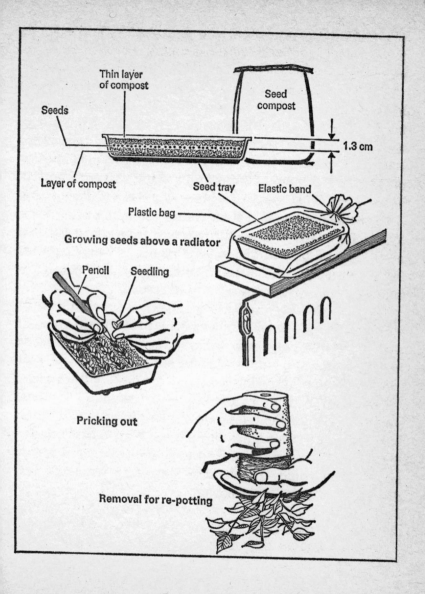

Thin layer
of compost

Seeds

Seed
compost

Layer of compost

Seed tray

1.3 cm

Elastic band

Plastic bag

Growing seeds above a radiator

Pencil   Seedling

Pricking out

Removal for re-potting

plant. As the plant grows, you will need to find a larger pot for it – the roots should just spread nicely into the pot without being too cramped.

You can check if the roots are growing so much the plant needs a new pot, by knocking out the plant. It's best to knock out the soil and the plants together. To do this, water the soil first, then hit the edge of the pot quite hard against a table or wall, for instance. Now turn the pot upside down and you should find the soil will come out all in one piece. Then you can replant in a new pot if necessary.

In the next chapter, I'll be telling you about other ways of growing plants – from cuttings and from roots. I'll also be telling you how to divide your plants and take cuttings for your friends. And later on in the book, you can learn about growing your own trees from seeds!

You may find the small seeds I mention here difficult to grow. So do quite a lot of older people! If you find yourself having trouble, why not try planting some larger seeds indoors which you can later plant out of doors?

You might try growing the following flowers from seed: French and African marigolds, dwarf dahlias, Cosmos, sunflowers. Plant these larger seeds first indoors in pots or boxes. When the seedlings begin to grow, you can transfer them to larger seed trays. And once the weather is warm enough you could try planting your new plants out of doors where they should flower.

New plants from old

I've described several times how your plant might grow so big you need to repot it or divide it. And I've also pointed out that, as your plants begin to grow well, you may want to give friends cuttings. This chapter is about just that, making some new plants from the old one.

Dividing your plants is easy if you take care not to disturb the roots too much. You will be able to tell when the plant needs dividing. In some plants, shoots will begin to appear at the bottom, near the roots, and you can turn each of these into separate plants. Mother of Thousands is one example of this kind of plant.

What you have to do is simple. First, knock the plant out of its pot as I explained in the last chapter. To do this, you have to water the soil first, tap the pot sharply against something hard, turn it upside down, and plant and soil should come away in one piece.

Now, you can gently pull some of the soil away from the roots so you can see what you are doing. Then pull away the new shoots *along with the roots which are nearest to them. Do this carefully*. The new shoots will, of course, need roots if they are to grow!

Now you can re-pot each of the new plants in fresh soil just as you did with the first one. Keep the plants around your house, or give one or two away to friends. Make sure you water them well and keep them well protected from cold and draughts at first.

The other way of giving new plants as presents to friends who want to grow plants, is to give them a cutting. The easiest kind of cutting for you to take is a stem cutting.

What you need

Your own plant
A new plant pot
A sharp knife

Cutting compost
Water

It is best to take a cutting about 7 cm. down from the tip of a shoot. Choose a shoot which looks strong. Then make a clean cut about 7 cm. down, preferably just below where a leaf joins the shoot. Pull off this leaf and any others just immediately above it. You will need a clear 5 cm. of bare stem to plant in the cutting compost made up of half sand and half peat or soil.

Then plant the new cutting in the compost as you did with the first plant. It will take a few weeks to make roots but then it should grow well.

You could spray the cutting gently with very lukewarm

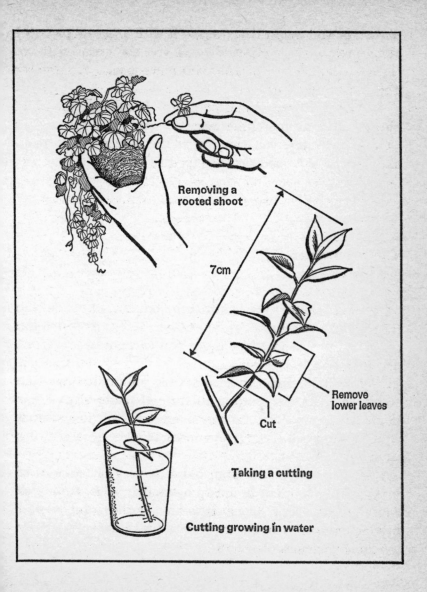

Removing a rooted shoot

7cm

Remove lower leaves

Cut

Taking a cutting

Cutting growing in water

water; or you might try covering it with a plastic bag, as I suggested doing with seeds when you are growing them. This is because your cutting will need special care during the first few weeks.

You can grow your cutting at first in another way, and this is probably more interesting. If you grow the cutting at first in water, you can watch the new roots develop. Busy Lizzie is a good plant to try this with.

What you need

A stem cutting   A glass
Clean tap water

Instead of planting your cutting in compost, just stand the cut end in a small glass or jar of clean tap water. Soon the roots will form and grow. Later you can pot up the plant as usual.

Some people prefer to keep adding soil gradually to the water till a proper potting mixture is made after a few days. But in any case, the new plant will have to go into a proper plant pot, large enough for it, once it is growing well.

Growing new plants from old is a very cheap way of making your room or house an attractive place. And once again, these plants when they have grown and started producing flowers or pretty leaves, make cheap but very welcome presents.

There are one or two other ways of producing cuttings apart from the one I have mentioned. You could take a cutting by breaking off a small stem and 'knuckle' from the main stem of your plant. Then pot it in the usual way. Try this with fuschias. Or you might have a plant which grows its own new plants – the spider plant, chlorophytum, is like this. You gently break off the baby plant and pot it up.

Cacti, too, can be propogated very easily in the soil. All you have to do is break off a small section – be careful of those spines! – and it will grow again into a new plant in moist potting soil.

Grow your own trees!

Did you realise you could grow little trees of your own in the house? The pips and stones you throw away from oranges, lemons, apples, grapefruit, can all be planted. With luck and care you should be able to grow small trees from them, though you won't produce any fruit.

Next time you eat an orange or apple, why not plant the pips? You will have to give them the best chance to grow by planting them in a good soil compost again. Try John Innes. Mix it about half and half with sand.

What you need

Potting compost
Some sand
Newspaper or a piece of
   glass

A plant pot
Pips from fruit
Water

Plant the pip just as you would another seed, covering it

lightly with compost. Then keep the pot in a really warm position. You must give the pip extra care. Try covering the pot or box at first with newspaper or a piece of glass. Growing pips and stones is much more difficult than growing ordinary flower seeds.

You will have to be extra careful, too, about keeping the plant well watered. If it is in a very warm position, the soil will dry out quite quickly. So check each day, feeling the soil surface to see if it is dry.

Because pips and stones are difficult to grow, don't be too disappointed if you are unlucky first time. To get a better chance of success, try growing a few pips at the same time. Put them in a large pot or seed box, and plant them as usual, quite spread out. A good help is to soak the pips for a day or two before planting them. Or you could try planting them in soil in a polythene bag, tied up, to keep them protected.

Which pips and stones make the best trees to grow? You can try tangerines. Tangerine plants have dark shiny leaves. Grapefruit, orange and lemon trees are pretty to have around the house, too. All of these seeds should be soaked overnight before you plant them. Apple, pear and plum trees are all fairly easy to grow, but don't try to plant them outside at a later stage. Trees grown from pips and stones inside the house are not very well suited to outside conditions. And often they are rather different from their parent tree.

It is best not to plant apple, plum and pear stones straight away. You could keep them in the refrigerator in some damp peat moss for a little time first. The moss and pips should be together in a jar. Turn them over from time to time until you see the pips start to sprout. Then plant them.

Another kind of tree you could try growing is the avocado. If you have avocado pears in your house you will know there is a very big smooth stone inside. Ask if you can have this. You will be able to grow it at first in water, and then later on in a pot. Its leaves are a little bit like a rubber plant's leaves, but not as glossy or thick.

What you need

Avocado stone

Tall jar or glass

Compost

Water

Plant pot

First of all, take the thin brown cover off the avocado stone. Then put the stone, which is actually a seed, in a glass or jar of water, so that it is suspended. Only the bottom, rounded part of the stone should be in the water so you will have to find a glass just the right size. The top of the stone, the pointed end, should stick out of the glass.

It takes a few weeks for the avocado to start roots, but once this happens they grow pretty fast. You will be able to watch them through the glass. Keep the glass in a fairly dark place at first. Then, when the stem begins to grow, you can bring it out into the light.

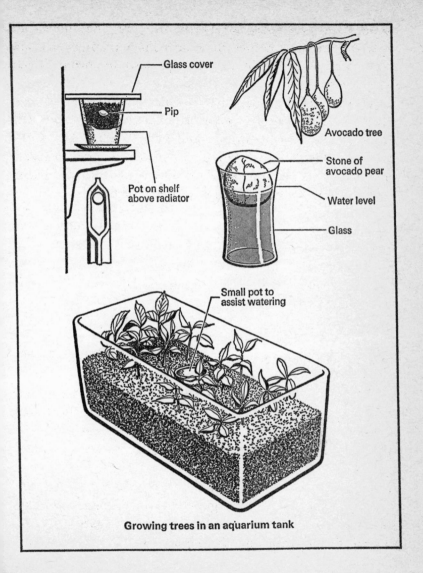

Glass cover

Pip

Pot on shelf
above radiator

Avocado tree

Stone of
avocado pear

Water level

Glass

Small pot to
assist watering

Growing trees in an aquarium tank

After quite a long time, about eight weeks, you will be able to put the new avocado plant in a pot with potting soil. By this time, it should have grown quite tall and have leaves. It is fun to watch a plant grow in this way and help it to change from a smooth round stone which you might have thrown away, into a pretty plant for the house. If you can't get avocados for this experiment, try growing an acorn in just the same way.

If you want to have different kinds of trees you have grown yourself, all in one place, you can plant the pips and stones in a large box or even in a tank you might normally use for fish. If you do use a tank, you should make a little hole in the middle of the soil and then put a small flower pot in the hole. You will be able to water the plants in the tank through this pot – it will help the whole tank to stay evenly watered.

If you want to try different kinds of trees in a box or tank, keep each kind in a separate row. Write out a label to say which plants are which. Although it is more difficult to grow plants and trees from the throwaway pips and stones, you will feel really proud if the plants actually grow.

A garden at your window

Now that you have learned to grow plants in pots and bowls inside the house, you can grow plants outside too. Even if you have no garden, you can grow flowers and other plants in a window-box. This is specially good for children who live in flats in a town, but children who have quite a big garden may still like to try making a window-box too.

First of all, think about what you will need for your box and how long and deep it should be. Window-boxes should be at least 15 cm. deep and probably a bit deeper. They should be the same length as your window.

What you need

Hardwood, 2·5 cm. thick
Some 5 cm. nails
Wood preservative
Broken bricks

Paint for the outside
Fine wire mesh netting
Brackets

You can buy seasoned oak, or some other hardwood for your box. Cut it to the right lengths to fit your window and plane it. (You may need your Dad to help here.) The two ends should fit inside the two lengths. Then you can join these together with the 5 cm. nails. You could make the box itself even stronger by screwing an angle bracket to the outside of the box at each corner.

Your window-box may not seem very heavy when it is empty. But once it is filled with soil and planted it could be very dangerous if it suddenly fell. *So you must fix it very securely.* You will need two strong iron brackets to fix the box to your window frame. If you fix your box to the wall for any reason, you will have to plug the wall at least 5 cm. deep before fixing the bracket. *Ask your Dad to check.*

One point here. Decide very carefully exactly where the box should go before you finally fix it. First of all, make sure you will still be able to open the window, even when the plants have grown! Secondly, make sure you will be able to plant and look after the window-box easily, either from inside or outside the house. If the box is at a ground floor window, you may be able to work on it from outside. If it is at an upstairs window, then you should be able to reach it easily and safely from inside the room.

Another point, too. Always fix the window-box in position *before* you plant it. It will be very heavy and difficult to fix once it is full of soil and plants.

But before you do that, soak the inside of the box with a wood preservative. Don't use creosote. This is especially

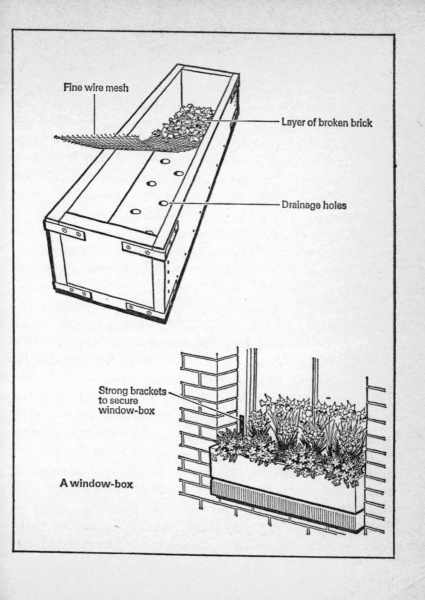

Fine wire mesh

Layer of broken brick

Drainage holes

Strong brackets to secure window-box

A window-box

important if you have used softwood. Leave it in the open for about 10 days, then paint it outside to suit your house. White or pale colours make a good background for plants.

Plants growing in window-boxes are not living in quite the same conditions as plants in the garden. You will have to give them drainage, and often some water. You can drill drainage holes in the bottom of the box, about 10 or 12 of them 1·3 cm. in diameter. Put fine mesh netting to cover the bottom of the box, and stop soil falling through. Then put down broken bricks over the actual holes to help the drainage.

You can now prepare the soil in which your plants will grow. A layer of turves, with the grass facing downwards, can go on top of the bricks; or you could put a layer of peat (moss peat). And then the box will be filled up with compost. Let this settle for a day or two before planting. Put a few pieces of charcoal in the soil to keep it smelling nice. If you prepare the box well, you should only need to change the soil every two or three years.

What plants can you grow in your window-box? Geraniums, pansies, primroses, hyacinths, daffodils are all good. If you want flowers all the year round, you will need to plant twice a year. You can plant in May to get the plants that flower during the summer. And you can re-plant in October with bulbs for spring. When you change the plants in the autumn you can dust the soil with a little hydrated lime to keep it sweet-smelling. In spring, you can add a small amount of bone meal to the soil.

Otherwise, there will not be much work to do in your window-box. Much of the time, rain will water the plants naturally, unless the eaves stick out too far. But in hot weather especially you will need to water them yourself very well indeed. Always check the soil to make sure, especially from about April until the end of the summer. Remember to take off any dead flower heads, too.

If you are going on holiday, you must give the window-box a thorough watering and soak first. You can then press a few small flat stones into the soil in between the plants – this will stop the water evaporating too fast in hot weather. A watering can is best for watering window-boxes.

In a later chapter I will be telling you how to grow things to eat in your window-box – mustard and cress, chives, parsley, and even lettuce!

Troughs, tubs and sinks

Perhaps you want a little more space to grow things than a window-box but you don't have a garden. If you have a back-yard, or a balcony, or even a little space just outside your front door, you can still grow flowers and even trees as you might in the garden.

What you need first is a container. One type of container is a stone or concrete one. It might be a big stone trough or just an old kitchen sink which someone has thrown out. You can turn this into a little garden.

What you need

A stone trough or sink

Some bricks

Small pieces of brick and
    stone

Old turves

Compost

Broken charcoal

If you are using a sink that is glazed, you must chip its

surface inside. This will make it more porous, so that water can soak in, and plants can cling to the sides better. If your trough has no drainage holes, you need charcoal to keep the soil sweet. Support your sink or trough firmly on the bricks, and make sure it is absolutely safe before you start preparing and planting it.

But before doing this, make the usual layer of broken bricks, then turves on top. Now you can make up the trough or sink with compost. When you have put in this soil leave it to settle for a few days before beginning planting. Then, if you like, you can plant it with the same kinds of things as in a window-box. This means planting bulbs in autumn, and summer-flowering plants in spring. But you will be able to plant more at once, and group them into a pretty garden scene.

Some good plants to grow in a trough or sink are primroses, pansies, geraniums, phlox. It is best to use little plants, which you have bought or grown in pots. Take care not to disturb the roots too much when you are planting them.

If you want, you can make a little rockery in your trough or sink. Use pretty stones, and set them well into the soil, to make your rockery. Try to make the rocks and stones look natural. You could then plant a few flowers like pansies and double daisies. You can buy special miniature bulbs, too, to grow in your trough garden.

It will be very nice if your trough or sink garden looks colourful all the year round. So choose several different types of plants which flower at different times.

Instead of a sink or trough, you might choose to grow things outside in a tub. The best thing to use for this is an old barrel or cask. See if your Dad knows where you might get one. You won't want a tub too tall or you won't be able to see the plants well or look after them!

The good thing about a tub is that it is usually deeper than a trough or sink so you can grow plants in it which need a greater depth of soil and more moisture round the roots. You can even grow certain types of apple and pear trees, and miniature and ordinary shrubs in tubs.

What you need

A barrel or cask, cut off to the right height	Turves
	Compost
Broken bricks	Bricks, wood or large stones

You will need to make holes for drainage in the tub, by drilling them as you did for the window-box. Once this is done, you can start with your layer of broken bricks, about 5 cm., and then cover these with a layer of turves. It is best if the turves are decaying a bit. This layer should come nearly halfway up the tub. Then you can make up the rest of the tub with compost in the usual way.

It is probably best, before you actually fill the tub, to get it firmly in its final position. Fix it securely on top of large stones, bricks, or wedges of wood.

Just as you did with the trough or sink, let the soil settle

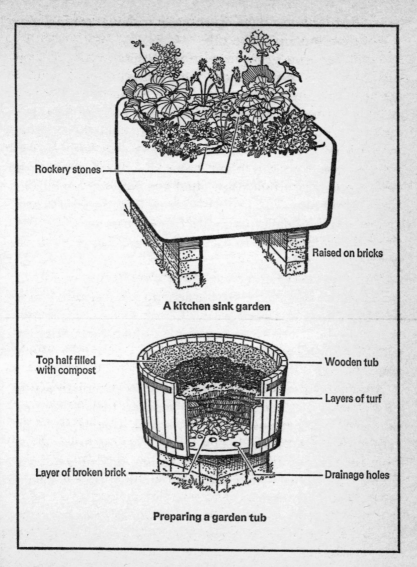

Rockery stones

Raised on bricks

A kitchen sink garden

Top half filled with compost

Wooden tub

Layers of turf

Layer of broken brick

Drainage holes

Preparing a garden tub

down first for a few days. Eventually it should settle about 5 cm. from the top of the tub.

What can you grow in a tub? Generally plants from about 15 cm. to nearly 70 cm. high. Some good ones would be begonias (grow the tubers in the house in spring and plant them in the tub at the beginning of June), dahlias (you can get dwarf bedding types, and again they can be grown from tubers in boxes inside the house), geraniums, marguerites. You can plant bulbs, too. As I mentioned before, miniature bulbs are good for growing outside in troughs and tubs. You could also grow large hyacinths and tulips, and the smaller daffodils. Schools can get up to 100 fir tree seedlings free from the Forestry Commission, to plant.

In each case, whether you use a trough, sink or tub to make an outdoor miniature garden, do not forget to check whether the plants need water. Check too for weeds and weed them out gently so you don't disturb roots of other plants. Nip off any dead heads. This won't take much time.

Although most of these containers will get enough water outside except in hot dry summer months, make sure they don't get too much water! Don't stand troughs, sinks or tubs right against the side of a house, to avoid heavy drips from the eaves. And for the same reason, don't have them under trees either – imagine snow melting after a heavy fall!

Sow and eat!

Did you know you can grow some things inside your house that you can eat? Not large plants like potatoes and broad beans, of course; but small plants that give a delicate but important taste to food.

You can grow mustard and cress to put in sandwiches and on salads. You can grow chives to beat into mashed potato, or whip into cream cheese. You can grow other herbs like parsley, thyme and mint to flavour food as it is cooking. You can also grow one or two salad plants quite well in a large window-box, such as lettuce and radishes.

Let's start with mustard and cress. You might have grown this at school on a wet cloth or even a plastic sponge. Anyway, here's how to keep a good growth of mustard and cress in your kitchen.

What you need

A seed box
Some fine soil
A plastic bag

Mustard seeds and cress
  seeds

Put about 5 cm. of the soil, which should be fine and not heavy, into the seed box. Then sow the cress seeds quite thickly on top of the soil. Don't cover the seeds but press them down into the surface. Then water the seeds well and cover them with a plastic bag which you can see through. You can now put them in a warm place like the airing cupboard (ask Mum again).

You need to plant the cress seeds first because they are slower to germinate than the mustard seeds. You can plant the mustard seeds in the same box with the cress about three days later. This means they should both be ready to cut at the same time.

You will soon be able to tell when the seeds have germinated and the seedlings are growing. When they are about 2·5 cm. high, you can cut them with small scissors, for eating. Just cut as many as you need. And if you keep sowing more seeds every two or three weeks, you will always have mustard and cress ready in the house for garnishing. I think your Mum will be pleased.

Mum would probably like the other things I have mentioned that you can grow to eat in the kitchen. It looks and smells nice, and is very handy, if you can grow one or two different herbs at the same time.

One way to do this is to grow each herb in a small separate pot, and have all the pots inside a window-box. In this case, the window-box can be inside the house. And if you like, you might try one of the white plastic ones, rather like a deep tray, which you can buy in the shops. You might put little plastic pots of herbs in this. Have two

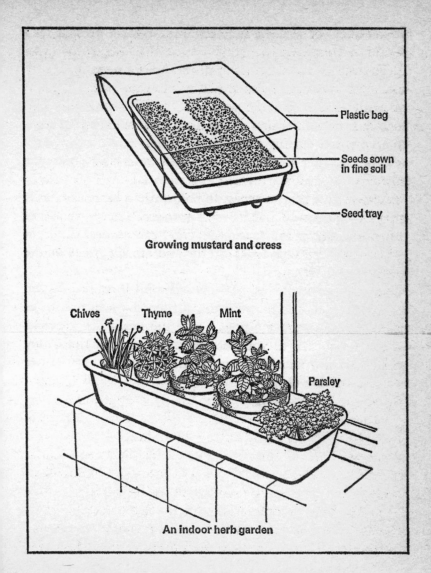

Growing mustard and cress

Plastic bag

Seeds sown in fine soil

Seed tray

Chives Thyme Mint Parsley

An indoor herb garden

if you like – or make a different one up for a present for a friend or your Gran or Aunt.

The herbs will stay warm in the house, even in winter, so keep them on the windowsill where they will get plenty of light. And keep them well watered. It is probably best to buy little plants first or get Dad or someone you know to give you a cutting from their garden. Soon, your herbs will be growing so fast that you will be taking your own cuttings too, and starting off new plants.

Always give mint a separate pot, quite a large one, as it grows very quickly and its roots wander. There are lots of different kinds of mint, and you can grow several different types together. This looks pretty and smells sweet in the kitchen.

You can grow chives, parsley and mint from seed if you want to try. Get some from the garden shop and plant as usual, each in separate pots. Once the herbs are growing well, keep cutting as you need them for cooking, and they will grow new shoots. If the plants grow too big, either re-pot or divide them.

Fun with seeds

So far I have talked mainly about how to grow plants that are pretty to look at or good to eat. But you can also have fun with plants and seeds, seeing how they grow. It's often easier to do this, if you are not trying to produce a lovely plant to give away!

One good way to watch how different seeds germinate and grow is to grow them on wet canvas! This is what you do:

What you need

A seed box or tray
Earth to fill it
Water
Canvas twice the width of
   the box

Dried peas, beans, lentils,
   etc.
A larger box than your
   seed box

Fill your seed box with earth, lay half the canvas on top of the soil, leaving the other half hanging ready to fold over. Now spread out your dried peas, beans, lentils and so on on top of the canvas. Fold the other half of the canvas back over the seeds. Damp the canvas well.

Now put the larger box over the seed box, so that the seed box and seeds are in darkness. Very soon the peas, beans and lentils will germinate and begin to grow. This way you can watch them grow, whereas you can't in a plant pot. Which seeds grow the fastest? What happens as they grow? You could try making drawings day by day or week by week.

Another experiment you can try is with two flower pots.

What you need

Two flower pots, one bigger than the other	Clay
	Water
Some seeds	

Put wet clay around the outside of the smaller plant pot. Now stick the seeds in this all the way round the outside. Cover the small pot and seeds with the larger pot, so they are in darkness. Put the whole thing upside down in a large bowl of water. In a few days, you will see the runners from the germinated seeds beginning to grow. In a short time, they will be so long they will hang down.

Do you remember when I told you how to grow trees from pips and stones? I said it was hard to grow apple, pear and plum pips straight away, but it helped to keep them in the fridge for a few weeks. Here is how to watch these pips growing into plants.

What you need

Apple, pear or plum pips or stones	Two pads of cotton
A jam jar	Water

Dampen one pad of cotton and put it in the jar. Then put your pips and stones on top. Cover them with the other cotton pad which you have also dampened. Then put the jar in the fridge. Don't put the lid on top.

If you keep the cotton pads damp, in a few weeks the pips and stones will start to sprout. The seeds will have germinated. You have to wait longer for results with this experiment than with some others. This is because these sorts of seeds must have time to ripen in a damp, cool place.

Another way you can watch different seeds sprout, but more quickly than the last experiment, is to grow them on a paper hanky!

What you need

A drinking glass	Water
A paper hanky	Some seeds

This time try growing sunflower seeds and corn, as well as peas and beans. Wet the paper hanky slightly then line the inside of the drinking glass with it. Then put about an inch of water into the bottom of the glass. This means the paper hanky will stay wet.

Now you must put the seeds carefully between the wet paper and the glass, so that you can see them from the outside. If you want the seeds to sprout fast, soak them first overnight.

Again, you will see that some seeds sprout faster than others. You might keep a diary, day by day, of how each seed is doing, or do drawings from time to time.

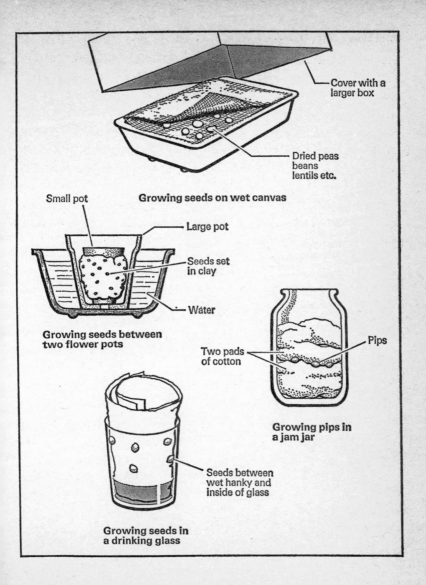

Cover with a larger box

Dried peas beans lentils etc.

Growing seeds on wet canvas

Small pot

Large pot

Seeds set in clay

Water

Growing seeds between two flower pots

Two pads of cotton

Pips

Growing pips in a jam jar

Seeds between wet hanky and inside of glass

Growing seeds in a drinking glass

Grow your own garden

Now that you know about sowing seeds, growing plants and taking cuttings, you can make your own miniature gardens for the house.

Don't think you can only grow plants in pots, indoors. Have you thought about a bottle garden, a garden of cacti, a garden in a kettle, or an indoor water garden? Here's what you can do.

Bottle gardens

What you need
A large glass jar or bottle
A lid for it that fits
Small pebbles
A cork

Potting compost
Two longish sticks
Some plants

Choose a pretty jar or bottle, and one that is made of clear glass so you will be able to see the plants well. You might choose a jar that your Mum has used for bath salts. Make sure the lid is a good fit.

First, you will have to wash the pebbles and then drop them carefully into the jar to just cover the bottom. Try tilting the jar or bottle so you don't crack the glass.

Now you have to get the compost and plants inside the bottle! How do you do that? If your bottle has a very narrow neck, you may need to make a paper cone to help you do this. But normally, you should manage with just the two sticks, and a cork.

In any case, pour enough compost into the jar to cover about 3·5 cm. Then ease your plant carefully into the bottle or jar with the help of your two sticks. You should make a hole in the compost with a stick and then put the plant in this carefully. To help you cover the plant's roots with soil and make it secure, use a cork on the end of a knitting needle, or a piece of wire.

Once your plant or plants are planted, and you might plant several different types, you must damp the soil with water and then put the lid on the bottle garden. This way, the water in the bottle will be conserved and the plants will be protected from smoke, dust and draughts. Your plants should grow quite happily like this for a few years without further watering. This will certainly be an easy garden to look after! But if dead leaves or flowers occur from time to time, you will have to nip them off gently with the help of the two sticks.

What might you grow in a bottle garden? Obviously

not plants that will grow too high. Some good ones to try are: ivy, lady fern, African violet, chlorophytum and mosses. Try feather moss or scaly spleenwort. Mosses and ferns grow slowly so are good for a bottle garden.

You could try all shapes and sizes of bottle gardens, but perhaps you'd prefer to make a desert garden in a large bowl? By this, I mean a garden of cacti. Remember that these are desert plants, so they need lots of sun and warmth. They are easy to look after in one way though – they don't need as much water as other plants. In fact, it can harm them very much if you overwater them.

You can grow cacti from seed – get a packet from the gardening shop. In this case, grow them in little pots in potting compost, with a few pebbles in the bottom of the pot for drainage. You can also take a section of a cactus and quickly grow a new one from it, again in a pot with potting compost.

Later, if you like, you can stand several of these little pots in a large bowl and pile pebbles or gravel around them to make it look like a garden. Or you can plant the various cacti in potting compost in a bowl and add a few pretty pebbles, shells and small rocks for decoration.

You could try growing the Christmas cactus which has bright pink flowers, or Lobivia which is round, with segments like an orange. Or instead, try opuntia bergeriana, otherwise called the prickly pear. Only some cacti flower, but even those which do may not flower until they are quite big. To make your cactus garden more interesting, grow several different types of cacti.

54

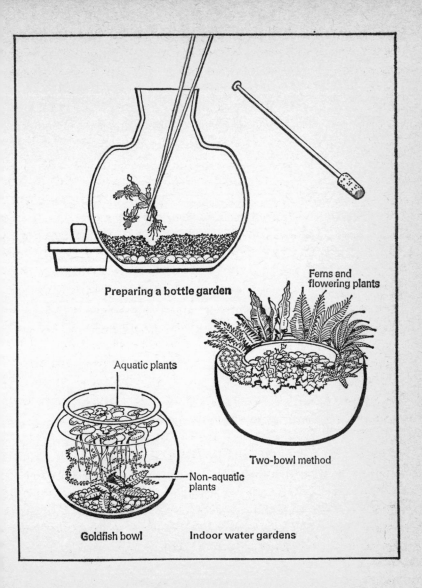

Preparing a bottle garden

Ferns and flowering plants

Aquatic plants

Non-aquatic plants

Two-bowl method

Goldfish bowl

Indoor water gardens

Indoor water gardens

In an indoor water garden you can grow all types of water plants. Some you will need to plant in soil, others will float on top of the water, letting their roots hang down underneath, just as water lilies do. Water gardens are easy to make and would look attractive in your own room. Or you might make one for someone in your family.

What you need

A goldfish bowl or deep
   dish
Pebbles

Sand or soil
Water plants of different
   types

Put a few pebbles in the bottom of the dish or bowl and then put in about 1·5 cm. of soil. You will be able to plant non-aquatic plants like ferns, by standing them in the soil. Put them in the goldfish bowl with two sticks, as you did with the bottle garden. Then pour in water very gently so as not to disturb these plants. You will need water almost to the top of your bowl. Now you can plant aquatic plants like Frogbit, which is a little bit like a small water lily. Other water plants include Canadian pondweed, water plantain and water forget-me-not.

Another way to make a water garden means using two bowls, one smaller than the other. Fill the smaller one with water and float aquatic plants in it. Put this bowl inside the larger one. Now you can fill the space between the two with soil and plant mosses, ferns and flowering plants, and add pretty pebbles to complete your water garden.

The important thing in making indoor gardens is not just to think in terms of pots and bowls. Try to get the best effect with several plants together. Put several pots in a large wooden box for instance so you get a whole range of plants.

Think about different types of containers. You can make miniature gardens in big old kettles, large teapots that have lost a lid. Some people grow tiny flowers like violets in a wine glass, or pretty tea cup. Suit the plant or plants to the container – and use your imagination!

Your own patch

At last your Dad's convinced you are a keen gardener and know something about it. He might decide to let you have your own patch in his garden, to grow what you like.

What you need

A spade   A hoe
A digging fork   A rake

If you are going to plant flowers and vegetables you will need a spade so that you can first of all thoroughly dig over the soil. Then you will need a digging fork with a long handle for forking over the soil so that it is loosened. You will need a rake to finish off making the soil fine for planting. And then, later, you will need a hoe to help keep down the weeds. Of course you will still need your watering can, hand fork and trowel, too.

Most of the main garden implements are now made in

junior sizes and are stocked at gardening shops and centres. So see if you can get some of these if your Dad's garden tools are too big and heavy.

Choosing your patch

If Dad lets you choose your patch see that it will get plenty of sun and that it is not too near large trees whose roots might get in the way. The size of the patch will affect the type of things you can grow, so think about this carefully. Try to get yourself some good decaying compost to help the soil to be prepared well.

What will you grow?

If you want to grow bulbs for spring you must buy bulbs for outdoor flowering. Plant them in September to October. Plant snowdrops, crocuses, daffodils, hyacinths, tulips. All of these should grow well.

For spring and summer flowering, you could try growing pansies, antirrhinums, double daisies. Always try to keep some colour in your garden, so plant flowers to bloom at different times of the year. Think of primroses, forget-me-nots, violas and scillas.

If you want to grow vegetables, radishes are fairly easy to grow from seed. Lettuces can be grown from seed too. It is best to sow these straight into the open ground. They should do quite well.

Herbs should be easy to grow, too. Make a separate

patch for herbs, to hold a bay tree, some parsley, thyme, rosemary, chives and mint. Cuttings can be taken from these and potted up from time to time for immediate use in the kitchen.

Later, if you want to be more adventurous, try sugar peas which you can get as seeds from specialist dealers. When these are fully grown you can eat the pods as well as the peas. But as your patch grows, you will want to branch out to try real peas, potatoes, carrots, parsnips, beans and even strawberries. Then you will need a book on outdoor gardening – and this is really where my job comes to an end.

Good luck to you in all the gardens you grow, inside and out!

Plants you can grow

Here is a list of plants you might like to grow. There isn't room to tell you about all the plants you can grow, but you can find out about others from a seed merchant's catalogue or a gardening book.

Indoor Plants

Begonia: These plants have pretty pink or reddish flowers and pointed leaves with jagged edges. You can grow them inside in pots, or in a window-box if you like. You should get plenty of flowers if you look after these plants well. A begonia needs plenty of water, especially when it is flowering, and also plenty of light. But don't keep it in direct sun, though you need to keep it warm.

Busy Lizzie: This is an easy plant to grow, and it grows fast. You should get flowers all the year round, and these are usually pink but might be red or white. It needs a lot of water in summer – sometimes it needs watering twice a day. But in winter it needs very little water. When you want to take cuttings you'll find you can root them quite easily in water, before potting. Keep this plant warm and give it light but no direct sun.

Coleus: Coleus is a nettle, but it doesn't sting. In fact it's rather pretty with purple or red leaves, edged in green. This plant will only live for one season, and during that time it will need lots of water and light. Keep it away from draughts. Pinch out the flowers when they die, and the stems which grow too long, to keep the plant a thick, bushy shape.

Cyclamen: This plant again has bright flowers – they may be red, purple or white. The leaves are also pretty. Keep the soil damp but water this plant from the base. It needs coolness, but no draughts. You could grow this plant in a window-box or a small garden, too.

Geranium: Geraniums need lots of sun but flower very well. Flowers are pink, white and red, and the leaves are pretty too. You can grow geraniums in pots, or outside in window boxes, tubs or in small gardens. They need plenty of water in spring and summer but only a little in winter. If you grow them outside in the summer, it is best to pot them and keep them inside in winter.

Mother of Thousands: As its name suggests, this is a plant which grows quickly. It has to be divided and trimmed regularly because it grows so fast. It likes to grow in the shade and to be kept cool. Water it well in summer but only a little in winter.

Primula: This is a pretty little plant which is easy to grow and quite cheap to buy. Keep it in moist soil, with good light but no direct sun. It needs to be kept fairly warm. This plant flowers through the winter until the spring and should last several years.

Spider Plant: This is a very easy plant to grow, too. It has glossy long leaves that spill over the pot and hang down attractively. Little spider plants develop at the end of the long leaves and can be cut off and potted. Spider plants need a lot of light but little sun. They like to be watered often in summer but not so much in winter.

Tradescantia: Another climbing or trailing plant. This is very easy to grow and has pretty purple, white and green striped leaves. It needs plenty of water in summer, but not so much in winter. It likes sun. To take a cutting is very easy with this plant – just break off a piece of stem at a joint, then push the cutting into damp soil in a pot.

Outdoor Plants

Antirrhinum: These can be massed together in a small bed, or planted in rockeries or in a tub or trough. Plant them where they are to flower, in autumn if you want flowers in spring. Or plant in spring for summer flowering. They look very colourful, being orange, yellow, white, red, and sometimes pink.

Double Daisy: These should be planted in autumn about 12·6 cm. apart. You can plant them in window-boxes, troughs or tubs, or in a small rockery. The small Rob Roy type or Dresden China will look good in these surroundings. You can divide the roots after the plants have flowered, to produce new plants. Set the new plants straight into beds. Double daisies always look pretty and flower for a long time.

Nasturtium: This can be grown even in quite poor soil. Sow in March, to flower in June. Then the flowers will stay right through till November.

Phlox: A good plant for a window-box, trough or very small garden. It will flower right through summer and autumn.

Polyanthus and Primroses: These are quite similar and are treated in the same way. Use them in a very small bed, in a trough, tub or window-box. They prefer the shade and grow well in towns as well as in the country. Produce new plants by dividing the roots in autumn or after they have flowered. These plants will flower for at least two years, sometimes more. The best time of all for planting is October and some kinds will bloom as early as January and February.

Violet: This plant likes shade too but grows best in the country. Smoky air is not good for it. It is best to plant these in a bed of their own, so their runners do not affect other plants. Plant violets 15·2 cm. apart for best results. Make sure they are kept well watered, especially in summer.

Wallflowers: A nice plant to grow, because of its bright flowers which have a nice scent. At the end of April sow the seeds in a small seed bed, properly prepared. Sow thinly and keep the soil damp. If you want to grow wallflowers in tubs and window-boxes you can get special dwarf types. Ask at the gardening shop.